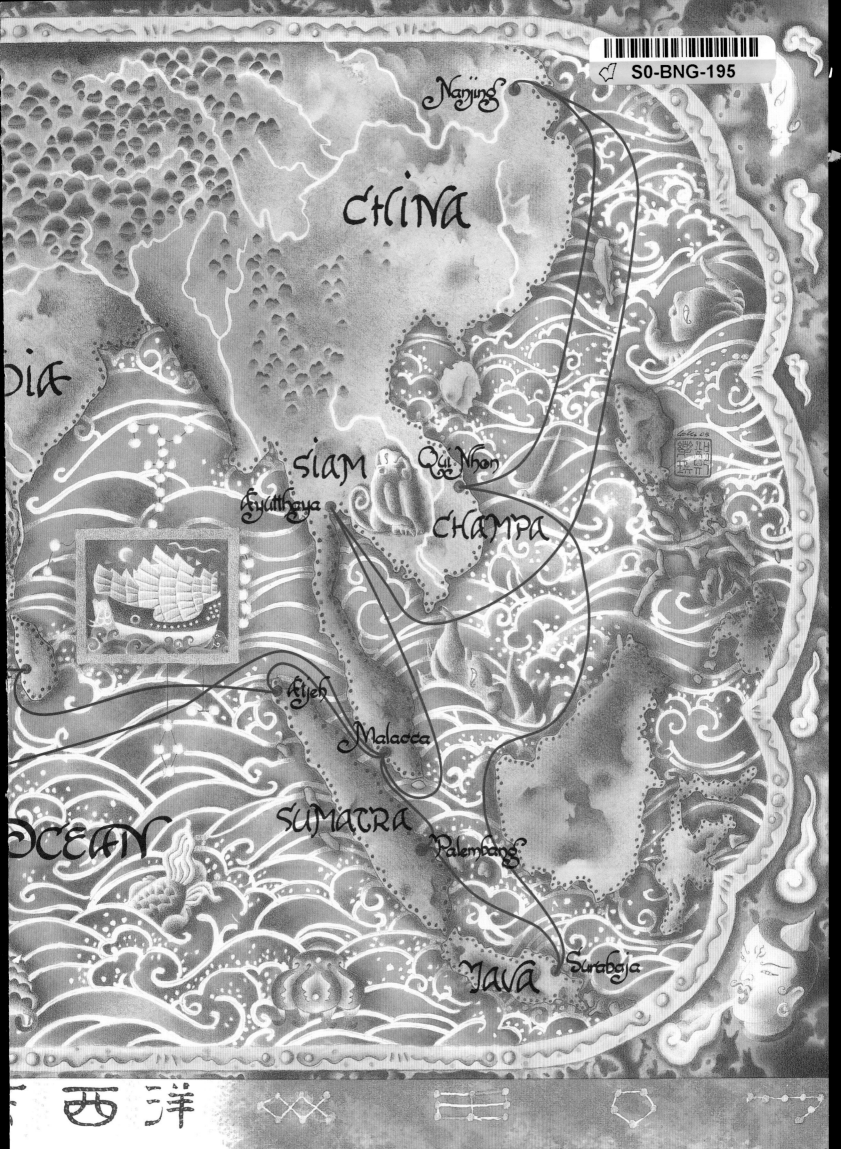

Nanjing

CHINA

INDIA

SIAM

Ayutthaya

Qui Nhon

CHAMPA

Atjeh

Malacca

SUMATRA

Palembang

OCEAN

JAVA

Surabaja

To my brother Tom, brave and loyal as the admiral himself. — Ann Martin Bowler

For Father, with whom all things are possible. And for the child in all of us. — L.K. Tay-Audouard

Author's note: *Adventures of the Treasure Fleet* is historical fiction. The story is based on seven Chinese naval voyages that took place between 1405 and 1433. Each event mentioned in the story actually occurred during one of the voyages, though fictional details have been added for the reader's enjoyment. At the bottom of each episode is a summary of historically agreed facts. Diaries of crew members and plaque inscriptions were the primary sources used in writing this book. Well-researched summaries of the voyages were also used. For the continuity of the story, all the voyages have been treated as one. Most, but not all, of the events mentioned in *Adventures of the Treasure Fleet* occurred during the first voyage. The storm, Saint Elmo's fire, pirate encounter, as well as the events in Champa, Java, and Calicut occurred during the first voyage, while the events in Malacca and Siam stretched over several voyages. The fleet first visited the Arabian Peninsula during the fourth voyage, and Africa was visited on the fifth voyage.

Acknowledgments: The author wishes to thank Eric Oey, Nancy Goh, Erin Dealey, John Stucky, and her family for their help and support on this project. The illustrator gratefully acknowledges Chung Chee Kit, Tan Ta Sen, Kim Jane Saunders, Julian Davison, Tan Guan Moh, Heng Kok Hiang for their invaluable help.

Published by Tuttle Publishing, an imprint of Periplus Editions (HK) Ltd, with editorial offices at 364 Innovation Drive, North Clarendon, VT 05759-9436, USA and 130 Joo Seng Road #06-01, Singapore 368357.

Text © 2006 Ann Martin Bowler
Illustrations © 2006 Lak-Khee Tay-Audouard
LCC Card No: 2006903177
ISBN 13: 978-0-8048-3673-9
ISBN 10: 0-8048-3673-6

First printing, 2006
Printed in Malaysia

10 09 08 07   5 4 3 2

DISTRIBUTED BY:
North America, Latin America & Europe
Tuttle Publishing, 364 Innovation Drive, North Clarendon, VT 05759-9436, USA
Tel: 1 (802) 773 8930 Fax: 1 (802) 773 6993
Email: info@tuttlepublishing.com; Website: www.tuttlepublishing.com

Asia Pacific
Berkeley Books Pte Ltd, 61 Tai Seng Avenue #02-12, Singapore 534167
Tel: (65) 6280 1330 Fax: (65) 6280 6290
Email: inquiries@periplus.com.sg; Website: www.periplus.com

TUTTLE PUBLISHING® is a registered trademark of Tuttle Publishing, a division of Periplus Editions (HK) Ltd.

Adventures of the Treasure Fleet
China Discovers the World

by Ann Martin Bowler

illustrations by L.K. Tay-Audouard

TUTTLE PUBLISHING
Tokyo • Rutland, Vermont • Singapore

Long ago the emperor of China called his old and trusted friend to his enormous palace. "I am now the most powerful ruler in the world," he announced. "We must show the world that China is the largest and richest nation on earth. We will build the greatest ships the world has seen and you, my friend, will command them. You will sail across the seas to befriend leaders of other nations, bring them gifts, and return home with fabulous treasures. This voyage shall bring great glory to China."

Zheng He was stunned. "Can I lead such a voyage?" he thought. "I have never sailed before! But the emperor saved my life in battle. I must be loyal to him now."

Bowing low, Zheng He replied, "Emperor, I am honored to lead this important voyage."

In the autumn of 1405, a massive fleet sailed from China under the command of Admiral Zheng He (pronounced "Jung Huh"). Over the next 28 years, the admiral and his fleet sailed more than 35,000 miles (56,000 km) exploring the vast "Western Oceans."

The admiral's beginnings were humble. When Zheng He was only ten his father was killed in a rebellion in southwest China and Zheng He was taken prisoner. This bright, tough boy soon had an unusual stroke of luck—he became the servant of prince Zhu Di ("Joo De"). In time the prince and

Zheng He grew to become close friends and the two of them fought to gain control of China. In 1402 they were victorious and Zhu Di was crowned emperor of China, becoming the third ruler of the Ming Dynasty. As emperor, he continued to rely heavily upon his old friend, Zheng He.

Zheng He was tall and stout, with "a voice like a huge bell" and skin "rough like the surface of an orange." His presence was commanding and his leadership made him perfect to lead the largest fleet the world had known on important voyages of discovery, commerce, and diplomacy.

China's emperor ordered hundreds of ships to be built and commanded that they be filled with valuable gifts and trading goods. The navy was so large it was named the "Treasure Fleet." The emperor appointed Zheng He as its commander, naming him "Admiral of the Western Seas."

Much of China was involved in the construction of the fleet. Beginning in 1404, more than 20,000 craftsmen lived and worked at China's imperial boatyards in Nanjing. Carpenters, ironsmiths, caulkers, sail makers, and many others toiled day and night constructing the huge fleet.

Soon all of China buzzed with activity preparing for the voyage. Loggers cut massive trees for the ships, carpenters sawed and hammered huge planks of wood, mapmakers drew long sea charts, weavers wove gigantic silk sails, farmers doubled their crops, and artisans crafted their finest wares. The emperor personally selected the finest gifts for kings of foreign lands. He toured the shipyards to exhort his shipbuilders. "Work faster men! The Treasure Ships must sail by winter!" he told them.

Secretly, the emperor was pleased, knowing he was building the largest and finest ships ever made.

Meanwhile, Zheng He studied his sea charts and sought advice from expert sailors. Though he sailed daily, he often lost control of his ship. And while others slept, the admiral worried, "Will I ever learn to control these gigantic ships?"

China's great shipbuilding expertise was used to build the largest wooden vessels ever seen. The ships were painted with tung oil, a waterproofing mixture that had been used since the 7th century. Dragon eyes were painted on the bow of each ship so that it could "see" where it was going.

To impress foreign leaders, the emperor ordered artisans to produce their finest wares. For the average Chinese, the voyages meant higher taxes and labor. But the emperor didn't notice. He was interested in the glory and riches the voyages would bring to his reign and to his country.

As winter approached, the massive ships were finally ready. Huge crowds gathered to see the ships be launched into the water. Then, thousands of crates filled with food, weapons, and trading goods were loaded on board, along with chests containing priceless gifts. At last, the sailors and soldiers boarded the ships. When the huge sails went up, the crowd cheered wildly. As the ships sailed downriver, people ran alongside waving bits of silk. "Be careful! Watch out for pirates and sharp reefs! We'll pray for you!"

Onboard the lead ship, Zheng He was thinking that no man had ever sailed this far. Filled with excitement, he lit incense and prayed, "With heart pure and true, I ask that our sails meet with favorable winds, that the sea lanes be peaceful, and that gold and pearls fill our ships with glory."

In the autumn of 1405, hundreds of brightly-painted junks were launched into the Yangtze River and sailed through China's capital, out to the open sea. With 317 ships and 27,000 men aboard, this was the largest navy the world would see until World War II, more than 500 years later!

Many important Chinese inventions made these voyages possible. The Chinese invented paper and printing. They also invented the magnetic compass and mechanical clocks. They studied the stars and mapped the major constellations. Zheng He's captains navigated using long paper sailing

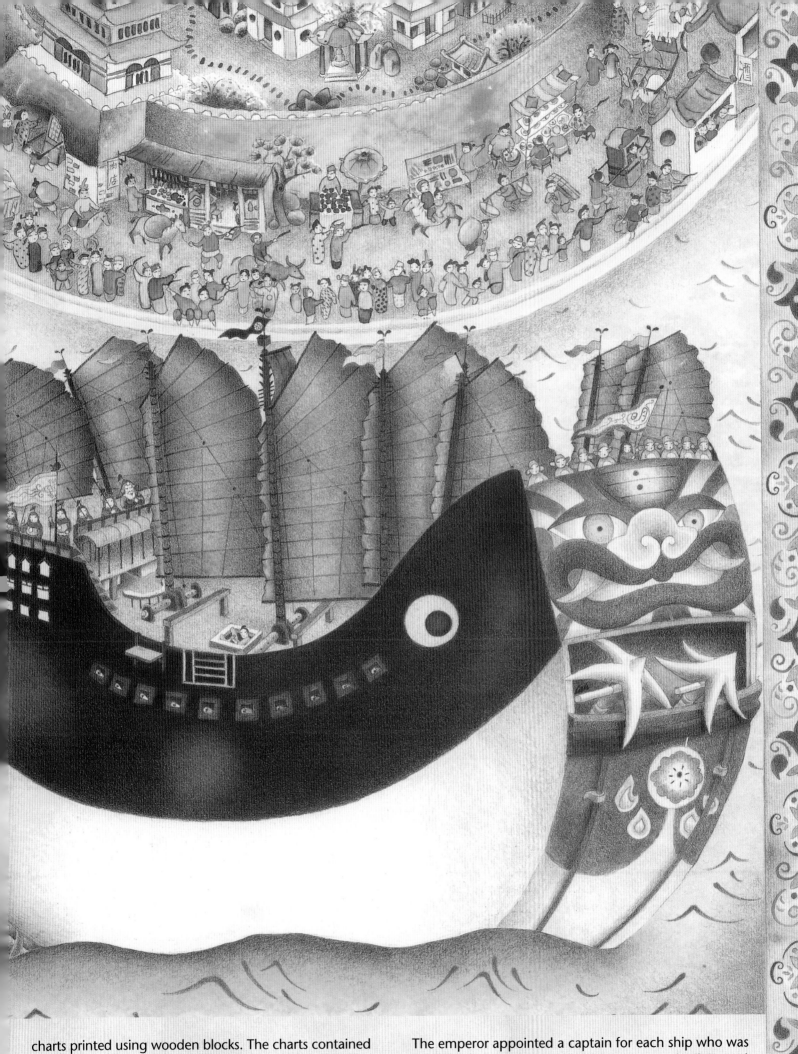

charts printed using wooden blocks. The charts contained compass readings, star locations, lengths of time, and important physical landmarks. Using these tools, the Treasure Fleet was able to sail across the open seas instead of hugging the coasts which was far more risky.

The emperor appointed a captain for each ship who was given the power "to kill or let live." Soldiers and sailors made up the bulk of the crew but doctors, scribes, shipbuilders, priests, cooks, and diplomats were crew members too. The fleet and its crew were truly an awe-inspiring sight!

China's gigantic fleet dazzled the people of Champa. The twelve largest ships in the fleet, called "Treasure Ships," were as long as one and a half football fields. No one has built wooden sailing ships as big before or since. By comparison, Columbus sailed to America 90 years later in ships that were less than a quarter the length. With nine staggered masts, twelve massive silk sails, and a complicated system for steering, the Treasure Ships could travel at eight knots per hour. Colorful paintings, bronze cannons, and elaborate carvings covered the length of each ship.

After days of fine, clear sailing, Zheng He sighted the rugged shore of Champa. Just then, powerful swells pushed the ships against razor-sharp reefs. "Steady the ships!" he ordered. While his men avoided the reefs, Zheng He studied his charts. "Man oars! I see a safe passage," he said.

When the fleet arrived, soldiers lined the shore, ready to attack. Zheng He's men prepared for battle but the admiral approached them calmly, "Greetings friends, we come in peace! We bring gifts from China's emperor." Much pleased, the king ordered the weapons to be put down. After days of feasting, the king led Zheng He on a tour of his realm, which was dotted with lovely temples and fertile rice fields.

Each Treasure Ship was like a city. Sailors slept on the lowest level, where the trade goods were kept. The middle level housed the kitchen, quarters for the officers, and an altar where prayers were spoken daily. The top level included a deck and an observation post used to calculate the ships' location.

After exchanging beautiful porcelains and silks for local ebony and ivory, Zheng He lavished Champa's king with gifts. Champa's ruler later sent elephants and a tiger to the Chinese court and Champa enjoyed close relations with China for many years to come.

The next port of call was Java, a tropical island with fire-spitting volcanoes. Java's port was one of the richest in the world, packed with traders from near and far. The admiral stayed for many months, exchanging lovely Chinese porcelains and silks for valuable cloves, nutmeg, and pepper.

Seeing that men young and old carried daggers at their waists, Zheng He approached a boy with an exceptionally handsome one. "Trade for your knife, boy?" The boy drew back in fear, but the admiral quickly offered him a handful of coins and said gently, "No need to be afraid, son." The boy's face lit up and in moments, the exchange was complete.

The boy then took the admiral's hand and pulled him into a yelling crowd to witness a tiger fight. The admiral enjoyed his time in Java, knowing he would soon sail across the wide Indian Ocean.

Scribes recorded details about each port the fleet visited—what the people wore and ate, their buildings and lifestyle. These records give us a glimpse of what life was like in Asia 600 years ago. Of their visit to the island of Java, the scribes noted that all men wore daggers at their waists, that the island's dense jungles were filled with long-tailed monkeys, and that the Javanese played lovely gamelan music. The travelers watched wayang plays, in which a performer unrolled a painted scroll while telling a story. They could not understand the words but were impressed that the

audience laughed and cried while listening to the tale. They also witnessed tiger battles and jousting contests.

Predictable winds made sailing in the Indonesian islands relatively easy. Over time, trade links developed with China, India, and Africa. With riches of gold, incense, and spices, Indonesia became an important center for trade. At the time of Zheng He's visits, Java was a very wealthy island. With fertile soils and reliable rainfall, the Javanese grew an amazing variety of crops. Merchants from many lands came here to trade for Javanese rice, pepper, and other products.

An ambitious young prince named Parameswara founded the trading port of Malacca around 1400. The town was located along the shores of the Straits of Malacca in what is now Malaysia, along the safest route linking China with India, Arabia, and Africa. Ships sailing through the Straits carried spices and other valuable trade goods, so Malacca was in the right location to become an important center for trade.

When Zheng He visited Malacca the first time however, the town was facing huge problems. Pirates attacked ships who sailed the Straits, and nearby ports in Sumatra and

Sailing north from Java, the admiral spotted fierce tigers, rhinoceroses, and elephants onshore. He also spotted a new settlement. "Lower sails"! he ordered. "That town's not on my chart!" On the shore a young prince greeted the admiral warmly, "Welcome to Malacca! Do you come here to trade?"

"I do. And I bring gifts from China's emperor," the admiral replied. But on entering the town, the admiral was puzzled. "Why are there so few traders here?" he asked.

The prince answered darkly, "Pirates attack the ships, so few dare stop."

"If we stop the pirates, may we land here often?" Zheng He asked.

"If you help Malacca, I will be loyal to China always," the prince replied.

"The pirates will bother you no more!" Zheng He promised, as he prepared to sail.

Siam threatened Malacca, wanting to gain control of its valuable trade. Parameswara was truly desperate for assistance at the time Zheng He's fleet arrived.

Zheng He and the prince took a strong liking to one another and agreed to become allies. Zheng He promised to use his fleet to eliminate pirates from the region and protect Malacca from its neighbors. In return, Parameswara became a vassal of China and pledged allegiance to the emperor. Under China's protection for the next 28 years, Malacca prospered, becoming the largest city in the region.

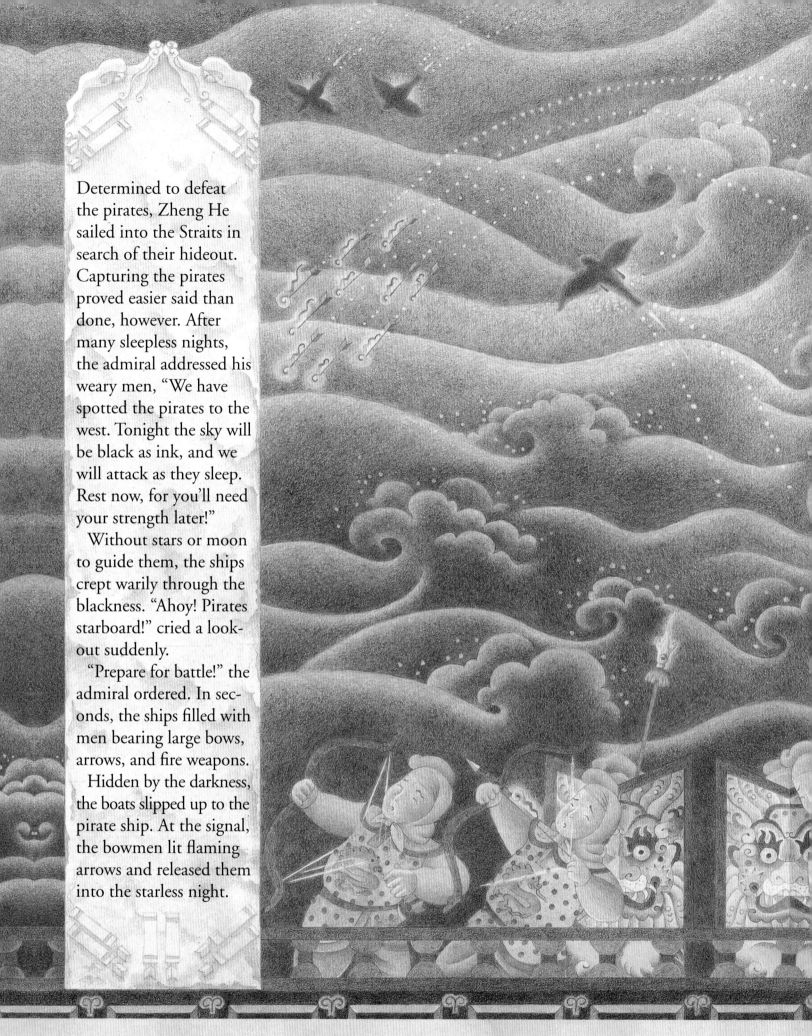

Determined to defeat the pirates, Zheng He sailed into the Straits in search of their hideout. Capturing the pirates proved easier said than done, however. After many sleepless nights, the admiral addressed his weary men, "We have spotted the pirates to the west. Tonight the sky will be black as ink, and we will attack as they sleep. Rest now, for you'll need your strength later!"

Without stars or moon to guide them, the ships crept warily through the blackness. "Ahoy! Pirates starboard!" cried a lookout suddenly.

"Prepare for battle!" the admiral ordered. In seconds, the ships filled with men bearing large bows, arrows, and fire weapons.

Hidden by the darkness, the boats slipped up to the pirate ship. At the signal, the bowmen lit flaming arrows and released them into the starless night.

The emperor had not ordered Zheng He and his men to fight but pirates were terrorizing ships throughout much of Southeast Asia at the time the fleet arrived and Zheng He decided to put a stop to the piracy in the Malacca Straits and make it safe again for trade.

The admiral and his crew battled the pirates in the Straits for many months. They eventually burned ten pirate ships and captured seven others. The pirate chief, Chen Zuyi, was captured and brought back to China for execution. Due to their efforts, travel and trade became much safer in

Southeast Asia for many, many years to come.

The Chinese developed many different types of weapons through long periods of continuous warfare. They invented the crossbow around 450 BC. Crossbowmen often began battles with a hail of short, deadly arrows.

The Chinese also discovered gunpowder in the 8th century. By the 10th century, gunpowder was used in fireworks and weapons. The Chinese invented guns, bombs, and mines. These weapons were not widely in use outside of China at the time, which gave Zheng He's fleet a huge advantage.

The Treasure Fleet was not sent to conquer distant lands, they came in peace. However, many of its crew were trained in military techniques. With as many as 300 different types of weapons aboard, the fleet was well prepared for battle. The weapons included flame-tipped arrows, "flaming tube missiles" that sent gunpowder and burning paper into an enemy's sails, and "gunpowder buckets" which were paper grenades filled with gunpowder. The soldiers were also equipped with traditional Chinese swords, knives, bows, and arrows.

The arrows struck their mark! Within minutes, the pirates' ship was in flames and they signaled surrender. Thinking the battle won, Zheng He's men cheered wildly. But the admiral was wary. "Board carefully men. I do not trust them." As the Chinese boarded the blazing ship, the pirates suddenly grabbed their swords and attacked.

Seeing this, the admiral lunged over the rail, intent on capturing the pirate chief. He barreled down the stairs after the chief, his voice as loud as a bell, "You are mine!"

"Ah no sir, you are mine!" the chief replied, swinging his sword.

Again and again their swords met. But with one swift blow, the admiral knocked the pirate's sword away and took him captive. After the battle, Zheng He turned the fleet to the west as the flaming pirate ship crackled and sank beneath the waves.

When fighting at sea, the Chinese gained an upwind position and then hurled explosives and fire weapons at their enemy. Crow's nests were manned around the clock to watch for enemy ships.

Communication between ships was important. During the battles, the ships used drums, flags, bells, banners, gongs, and lanterns to communicate. Drums or gongs were used to warn of storms or dangers. Lanterns were hung out at night or during foul weather and carrier pigeons were used for long-range communications.

17

Chinese ships had never crossed the broad Indian Ocean before. The seamen heard rumors of enormous sea monsters and wild seas. Undeterred, Zheng He commanded, "Raise every sail!" Later, he prayed at his altar, "Protect us across these wild, uncharted waters!"

Good luck sailed with the travelers. After three months at sea, the fleet arrived safely in Calicut, on the coast of India.

Greatly relieved, Zheng He rushed off the ship, only to be greeted by armed and angry soldiers. "What business have you here?" they asked.

"I bring gifts from the emperor of China," he replied, showing them a silk sash. The king of Calicut was very pleased, and brought the visitors to his royal storehouse. As big as a cavern, it was filled with pepper, incense, and cinnamon.

Located near the tip of the Indian peninsula, Calicut's market was large and prosperous. The Chinese were interested in Calicut's gemstones, pearls, and incense. But even more than that, they wanted to obtain spices like cinnamon, ginger, and pepper that were abundant here. Finding Calicut's merchants honest and its market filled with an astounding variety of goods, the Chinese stayed for many months.

Once again, the Treasure Fleet created quite a stir when it arrived. Calicut's ruler presented the travelers with sashes made of spun gold studded with pearls and gemstones.

Using gourds and copper wire, they performed music that was "extremely pleasant to the ear."

With the goal of obtaining the best wares produced in foreign lands, the Treasure Fleet was filled with China's finest products. Zheng He discovered that foreign kings greatly admired China's porcelain plates, cups, and vases as well as their amazing silk. Thousands of bolts of richly colored silk were packed into the holds of the giant ships. Iron, gold and silver coins, salt, tea, wine, books, nails, needles, pots, and candles also filled the ships.

On the first three voyages, the Treasure Fleet turned homeward after reaching Calicut. Greatly pleased by the results, the emperor commanded Zheng He to travel further. On his next voyage, he visited the Arabian port of Hormuz. The emperor asked the admiral to bring back exquisite pearls, rubies, diamonds, and emeralds that were readily available in the city's large marketplace. The travelers found Hormuz wealthy and well-kept. Fervent Muslims, the people prayed five times a day, did not drink or sell wine, and the women wore head coverings, as they do today.

"Diamonds! Emeralds! Rubies!" called traders from many lands in the Arabian port of Hormuz, the travelers' next stop.

"Hormuz truly is the gem of the world!" the astonished admiral said. "I will buy jewels of every description, but first I must buy precious pearls for my emperor."

In the city's largest shop he found a string of pearls glowing like diamonds. The admiral handed a few gold coins to the well-dressed owner. "You must be joking!" the man said, asking Zheng He to add coin upon coin to the pile.

"You are a shrewd trader!" said the admiral. "I surely overpaid but my emperor will love these gorgeous pearls!"

With the jewels safely stowed, the travelers sailed down the long African coast in search of strange and dangerous animals.

On the fifth voyage, the fleet traveled to other Arabian ports and one group visited the holy city of Mecca. The travelers saw religious and cultural practices quite different from their own. The people they met lived simple lives. Though the Chinese generally regarded foreigners as "barbarians," they were respectful of all religions and curious about life in other lands. Buddhist and Muslim leaders traveled with the fleet as diplomats. After the first voyage, Zheng He helped to establish a school in China to teach foreign languages, which continued for many centuries.

In the African village of Malindi, Zheng He was astonished to see lions, leopards, and zebras for the first time. "Such remarkable animals!" he declared. But he was even more surprised to see a giraffe. "Fantastic! This animal has heaven's gentle spirit. If I can take one back, it will greatly please the emperor."

Hearing this, the chief of Malindi replied, "The giraffe and other animals will be a gift for China's emperor if I may present them to your ruler."

"China is much farther than you imagine," replied the admiral, "but we are delighted for you to come with us."

While being led to the ship, the giraffe kicked wildly with his powerful hooves but was finally lured aboard. With all the animals safely on the ships, the fleet began its long homeward journey.

Sailing down Africa's coastline, the travelers saw tall mud huts surrounded by lush orchards. African lions, leopards, ostriches, and zebras amazed the Chinese but they were most astounded by the giraffes! One goal of the voyages was to collect rare and precious objects. Strange animals were especially important to the Chinese, who persuaded their African hosts to send a giraffe as a gift to the emperor. In the Somali language, the word for a giraffe is similar to the Chinese word for a unicorn which helps to explain why, when the animal arrived in China, some Chinese believed

that it was actually a legendary unicorn!

Many Africans were intimidated by the size of the Treasure Ships and did not invite them into their ports. Used to much smaller boats, it is no wonder they were frightened! But many others welcomed them warmly. Some historians believe that the fleet circumnavigated the globe but we will leave that debate for others. What is certain is that the Treasure Fleet visited over 30 countries including present-day Vietnam, Singapore, Malaysia, India, Sri Lanka, Saudi Arabia, Indonesia, Thailand, Somalia and Madagascar.

After Zheng He's first visit, Malacca's Prince Parameswara traveled to China in 1405. During his visit, the emperor gave him an official seal that proclaimed Malacca an outpost of the Ming empire. But Malacca's neighbor, Siam, believed Malacca belonged to them. The king of Siam captured Parameswara and snatched the official seal. Outraged, the emperor ordered that the seal should be returned and Parameswara released.

Diplomatic ties between China and Malacca grew stronger with each voyage. The Chinese built a fort in Malacca

By now, the ships were overflowing with precious gems, spices, and gifts for the emperor so the fleet headed homeward. Stopping in Malacca, the admiral was amazed. "Malacca is huge! The port is packed!"

"It is because you banished the pirates!" the prince told him. "How may I repay you?"

"May we build a fort here?" Zheng He asked.

"Of course, my friend!" the prince replied. As the fort was being built, the prince told of his trip to China. "We were treated well by your emperor! He gave me a beautiful seal. But on our way back, the king of Siam took the seal away from me!"

"That is not right!" the admiral said firmly, "The king of Siam will hear from us!" When the Malacca fort was completed, Zheng He sailed swiftly to Siam.

which they used to keep provisions, trade goods, and gifts.

Under Chinese protection, Malacca developed quickly. In just three years, the population grew to 200,000. It became a wealthy and powerful hub for international trade and was one of the largest cities in the world at the time.

As a strong and prosperous port city, Malacca controlled the trade in the Straits for many years to come. Once the Chinese fleets stopped visiting after 1433, Parameswara converted to Islam and the city became a leading center for the spread of the new religion in the region.

Arriving in Siam, Zheng He stormed into the palace like a tiger. "You, king, must treat Malacca well. If you do, China will reward you as a friend. But if not, we will treat you as an enemy."

On hearing this, the king became very angry. "You fool! Who are you to speak to me like this?"

"I speak for China," replied the admiral. "And my navy stands behind me. Come, let me show you." Outside, thousands of Chinese soldiers stood ready and huge Treasure of ships filled the harbor. At the signal, they fired flaming cannon balls over the palace.

The king was stunned. "Stop firing! Siam is a friend to China, too!"

"Good!" replied Zheng He. And from that day forward, Siam was a good neighbor to Malacca and sent regular tribute to China's emperor.

The fleet's next stop was the kingdom of Siam, a fertile land with many followers of the Buddhist religion. The king of Siam rode a white elephant while shaded by an elegant, gold-colored umbrella. Women made many decisions about trade and law and generally enjoyed much freedom.

Siam sent diplomats to China in 1407 with gifts of parrots, peacocks, and elephants. These pleased the emperor but when the Siamese snatched the seal from Malacca's prince, China demanded that Siam to stop harassing Malacca. Confronted by a well-armed fleet, Siam had no choice but to comply.

Zheng He's final expedition left China in 1432. It was the largest and most ambitious voyage and explored many Arabian and African ports. At this time, the aging emperor and his admiral erected stone tablets listing the fleet's accomplishments. The tablets said, "We have visited western regions, more than 30 countries large and small. We have traversed more than 35,000 miles of vast seas and beheld waves like mountains rising sky-high. Countries beyond the horizon have become subjects…and come bearing precious gifts for the emperor."

During their homeward voyage the fleet encountered a violent storm. The crew, believing that evil water dragons had come for them, called out to Tianfei, the patron goddess of sailors. Just when all seemed lost, a "divine light" touched the tip of a mast and within minutes, the storm subsided. In the words of the admiral, "As this miraculous light appeared, the danger was appeased." What they saw was a Saint Elmo's fire, static electricity that illuminates the sky with a blue-green glow. Occurring at the end of a storm, Saint Elmo's fire has often been interpreted by sailors as divine in nature.

As the fleet departed, clouds gathered and the seas grew wild. That night, fierce winds tossed the ships and several men were washed into the churning sea. "Tianfei, sweet goddess of the sea, save us!" they cried.

With his ship crashing through enormous waves, Zheng He thundered, "Turn into the wind! Ride the crests of the waves."

Then a swell as high as a mountain washed over the ship and the admiral was certain the end was near. "Spare us!" he cried.

Just then, a ray of light pierced the sky and filled it with brilliant colors. Then, the winds died and the ocean calmed. After prayers of thanksgiving, the ships headed north through sparkling seas toward home.

The Treasure Ships could weather storms like these due to numerous Chinese innovations. V-shaped hulls filled with rocks and huge rudders on the sides provided stability and accurate steering. Bamboo battens stiffened the sails, and allowed them to be furled in high winds. Modeled after stalks of bamboo, the thick hulls were divided into water-tight compartments and could withstand leaks and the impact of sharp reefs. Zheng He was so grateful that his ship survived the storm that he ordered the construction of a temple for Tianfei when he returned to China.

When the Treasure Fleet arrived at the capital, the emperor himself rushed out to greet it. Kneeling before him, Zheng He said, "My Lord, the voyage was a great success, and I have much to tell you. But first I must show you what we have brought!"

Cases and cases filled with jewels and many astonishing treasures were laid at the emperor's feet. A huge crowd struggled to get a peek. Leopards, lions, and zebras were brought out and the crowd gasped. "These are a sight to behold!" the emperor said.

Then a giraffe lumbered off the ship toward the emperor and the crowd grew silent. Thinking it was a magical unicorn, they bowed low as the creature passed. "This is fantastic!" cried the emperor. "It is a sign that Heaven truly looks favorably upon me and my kingdom. Tonight, we must celebrate!"

Each time the Treasure Ships returned to China they were filled with valuable spices, herbs, incense, dyes, medicines, gold, silver, gemstones, pearls, ivory, and many other rare items. The emperor was elated as Zheng He and his men laid treasures from as far away as Arabia and India at his feet.

The emperor had never seen a leopard, lion, ostrich, or a zebra and was astonished by their arrival. When the giraffe arrived in China in 1415, the emperor's assistant identified it as the fabled unicorn, an animal associated with peace and prosperity. The emperor expressed great pleasure and

officials bowed low before the animal and showered Zheng He with praise.

Ambassadors from many lands accompanied Zheng He back to China to pay tribute to the emperor. To show their respect, they presented elaborate gifts and bowed to the floor nine times. These ambassadors were given valuable gifts to bring back to their kings. And if the emperor favored a ruler, as he did Malacca's prince, he gave the ambassador a seal which confirmed the ruler's authority and made them an official part of the Ming empire.

At dusk, the ambassadors from many nations gathered in the emperor's massive hall to celebrate. They enjoyed fine food and drinks as entertainers flipped and twirled. But throughout the festivities, Zheng He sat quietly. As dawn approached, he finally spoke, "My Lord, our voyage was a wonderful opportunity to meet people from other lands. Yet during the storm, I was not sure we would live and vowed not to sail again. Tonight, I am restored and stand ready to sail again for China!"

"Then for China you shall sail!" the emperor replied, his eyes sparkling. Raising a cup, the emperor called a toast, "To more voyages, that will bring great glory to China!"

Lifting their cups, the guests replied, "To China!"

Epilogue

Over the course of 28 years, Zheng He led seven great expeditions that sailed further than anyone thought possible. From the Treasure Fleet's explorations of the "Western Oceans," China gained wealth, medicine, and knowledge. With each voyage, China's power and influence grew. Chinese culture spread to every port it visited. A century before Europe began its age of exploration, China was poised to become a colonial power.

But in 1424 the powerful and ambitious Yongle Emperor died. He is remembered for his many domestic improvements and for defending his nation against invaders. Even more, he is remembered as the creator of the magnificent Treasure Fleet.

China's new emperor commanded the voyages to stop but eventually agreed to a seventh voyage. However, during the homeward journey on this voyage, Zheng He died.

Admiral Zheng He was a brave and capable commander. He was the emperor's loyal friend and a devout man. The admiral's words about the voyages reveal much about this fine man. "Our fear was not to succeed. But if we serve our ruler with loyalty, then all things are successful. If we serve God with utmost sincerity, then all things are good."

With both Zheng He and the emperor gone, there was no longer support within China for overseas adventures. Thinking that the fleet was wasteful and expensive and only drained China of her vast wealth, China's new rulers no longer allowed overseas travel of any kind. The Treasure Ships fell into disrepair and no new ones were built.

China's new leaders were less adventurous than the Yongle Emperor. Turning their attention inward, they focused on domestic problems and issues. How different the world might be today had China continued its exploration of the world!